truths.
and freedom.

a memoir in poetry and prose
brandie freely

Copyright © 2017 Brandie Rogers

All rights reserved. No part of this publication may be reproduced, distributed, or transmitted in any form or by any means, including photocopying, recording, or other electronic or mechanical methods, without the prior written permission of the publisher, except in the case of brief quotations embodied in critical reviews and certain other noncommercial uses permitted by copyright law.

ISBN-13: 978-1-945532-49-8

Published by: Brandie Rogers

Cover & Book Construction by: Opportune Independent Publishing Co.

Edited by: Dr. Genovia Holmes and Eric Michael Ward

Printed in the United States of America

For permission requests, special orders or more information contact Brandie Rogers at bfree@brandiefreely.com

for solona.
you. are the best part of my story.

this work is also dedicated to my ancestors. the ones who dreamed. the ones who had stories to tell, but no way to write them. songs to sing, but nowhere to sing them. this book is dedicated to my ancestors, who like me had great imaginations and ideas of who they might become. for my ancestors whose dreams went unrealized.

i feel you. i remember you. i acknowledge you. i channel your spirit. and i am lifted by it. thank you for surviving. i learned how to from you.
i pray i make you proud. i pray i am your dream realized when you look upon me. i will sing for you. i will write for you.

you will forever be alive in me.

introduction.

most of the time i can hardly believe the story of my own life.
other times i ask myself if i've lived this way on purpose.

and then sometimes i wonder
if maybe i'm in love with plot twists. am i just not a fan of the predictability of traditional storylines? is it possible that i've lived on the edge just to keep things interesting? do i seek to be mentioned amongst timeless protagonists whose triumphs remain relevant for ages? or do i fear the thought of going into history stamped as ordinary?

i don't know.

maybe i am ordinary. and maybe my story isn't so unthinkable after all.

maybe it's just that i've dared to tell it. maybe i'm an ordinary woman with an extraordinary ability to walk brazenly in her truth.

maybe.

but for sure, i know this: i don't always need all the answers, and the answers don't always matter.

in the matter of my life
it all comes down to freedom. the freedom to really live.

and freedom is a process. it's not like i woke up one morning and decided i was going to be free. it took

truths. and freedom

a lot of soul searching. it took some pain and a lot of tears. i had a lot of questions, and had a hard time with some answers. i had to learn the purpose of forgiveness, and release. freedom takes time.

time, the essence of all things.

and most of all, this freedom i desired required truth.

without truth, there is no freedom.

this kind of truth is found buried under years of lies, so it must be dug up. it must be pondered on. it will not be easily revealed.

there is an art to this kind of truth.
and an art to this kind of freedom.

the first step is to go back to the very beginning.

brandie freely

i've kept a journal since the second grade. it was a yellow cardboard flip pad. you know, the one bound by wire at the top with green lines going across the pages. i can remember the shape of the round, uneven letters i wrote. i can only imagine what my eight-year-old mind thought was important enough to chronicle. i misplaced it long ago when we moved from my childhood home, and all these years later i still feel as if a part of me was lost. it sounds crazy, but the words on those lines mattered to me then, and they matter to me now. even then, god was sharpening my gift. hm. it's pretty amazing, actually.

over the years, i've penned just about every meaningful experience in my life. falling in love, emotional highs and lows, the birth of my daughter, being proposed to, getting married, and getting divorced. it's all recounted in one of several volumes of journals i've collected over time.
some years my journals overflowed. some years the majority of the lines were empty.

it never failed that i filled my journals the years i was in love.
every account of was explicit in detail. i wrote out each experience just as i remembered it. each stroke of my pen painted a picture of passion. in color.

i craved the emotions writing evoked. i'd cry and write, laugh and write, discover myself through reflective writing, solve problems in writing, be liberated by writing, be able to let go through writing. i'd even fall in and out of love as i'd write. scribing my own life offered me immense joy, and allowed me to channel

truths. and freedom

immeasurable pain.

shelves of journals in my home hold the exclusive accounts and details of various epochs in my life, each one an irreplaceable extension of me.

so.
after being married for three months and coming home one day to find that the one journal i'd cherished more than all the rest had been intentionally ripped to shreds, nearly ripped my heart out of my chest right along with those pages.

that's where the fall began.

let's go back:

for three months i'd been someone's wife.
i'd been out of college for six months and a
homeowner for five. we'd only been together about
half a year when he bought the ring. he would propose
a bit later at the twelve-month mark, and i would say
yes, because well…
it was the right thing to do. he was a great guy. well
spoken, educated, good family, great career. we had fun
together. he respected me. i felt safe.
and wasn't it better to marry than to burn? i'd heard
that growing up in church, which has a lot to do with
why i'd been striving to do right as far back as i could
remember. i wanted to do right, live right, and be right.
and make my parents proud. to hear 'well done'.

we were married six months after the proposal: june
of 2007

i don't remember praying about it one time.
don't recall stopping to even ask myself if it was what i
really wanted.
i didn't need to. marriage is mostly every little girl's
dream.

problem was: i wasn't a little girl anymore.

i was three months his wife when he invaded my
personal space and property, accused me of being
a deceptive liar, and ultimately tore the pages of my
journal out and ripped them apart.
i'm pretty sure that was when i snapped out of the
perpetual motion toward this contrived idea of

truths. and freedom

righteousness i'd been trying to hold on to. all at once, my heart was awakened. i could feel it pounding and hear echoes of it begging me to acknowledge it was there.

i had been ignoring the pounding. and muting the sound so i wouldn't hear it beckoning me to follow. i'd been drowning it out with lies about how perfect my textbook life was. i'd been drowning it out because if i followed my heart, i knew where it would lead. and that place was a dangerously far cry from the security of home.
so i ignored my heart. purposefully.

and had that journal remained closed, my heart may have never awakened, and i might still exist in that forged version of myself.

when it was opened at the hands of my enraged husband, it unleashed untamed emotions and forced me to confront them unexpectedly. the open book unveiled unfinished chapters from my past. it's no wonder he tore the pages, for they exposed my heart. they revealed who truly held it.

and that very offense, the literal act of destroying the contents
of my heart would only cause me to spend the subsequent years of our marriage desperately trying to piece those pages back together again.

i never got over it.
only pretended i did, because that's what i was good at. i'd learned how to be a great pretender long, long before then...

let's go back even further.

truths. and freedom

truths.

eventually, the desire to understand our own layers deepens. some dig in and do the work, getting down to the root of who they really are. some prefer not to bother with what's below for fear of altering what appears to be thriving above the surface.

i chose to dig for freedom's sake. this is my dirt.

truths. and freedom

my father told stories in front of a church congregation
every week.
the audience was always captivated.
including me.
he was a great story teller.
one of the best i've ever heard.
but
daddy never read
stories to me at night.
and i
never
got over it.

brandie freely

i told myself you loved me,
because you never did.
had conversations with myself.
made up excuses for you.
made your lack of affection okay in my mind.
told myself
of course you thought i was beautiful
because
you were daddy
and all daddies think their daughters are beautiful
and all daddies love their daughters
even if they never say it.
i made it all okay in my mind
so that i could mask the sadness.
i thought the world of you, daddy
i still do.
and still
i tell myself you love me
because you never do.

truths. and freedom

a girl needs a father
to be the example
of what love looks like
so she doesn't go out into the world
searching
for something
she won't be able to recognize.

brandie freely

i read romance novels
far too soon.
the passion
fell off the pages
and into my dreams.
and that is where
i learned
what love
is supposed to feel like.

truths. and freedom

and
i found definition
in the words
that rolled
off the tongues
of men who
got close enough
to whisper them
in my ear.

lost.
not knowing
yourself
feels like
standing in front of a mirror
staring
at a stranger
trapped
inside a body
that is
hard and cold
when you place
your fingers on it.
an image you can
touch
but not feel.

-self reflection

truths. and freedom

i searched all over for it
because i was desperate
for it,
but i couldn't
find it:
my worth.
so i began
operating in
inadequacy.
never really feeling
like enough.
as a result i wasted a lot
of time
searching instead
for validation
in
all
the
wrong
faces.

and when i couldn't,
i wanted to
depend on
you
to help
me
find what i was missing.

truths. and freedom

there
were
wounds
in
my
way.

and so i determined my worth
using relationships
as the measure.
the more he wanted me,
the more valuable i was.
and i would become whoever
he needed me to be
as long as he kept me around
so that i would know
i was worth something, anything
at all.

truths. and freedom

i was lost in insecurities i didn't know i had, which
meant i was even more lost than i didn't even realize i
was. i was in a black hole seeing false light somehow,
thinking i knew where i was headed, when that was
impossible.
how could i know where i was going when i was blind?

with no one to
hold my hand.

at fourteen i experienced my first hit of love.
i was an addict
instantly.
i had to have it.
i was obsessed with the high, and i preferred my hits dangerously potent.
i wanted the highest high.
but the effects of that
were that the lows were much lower.
i was willing to risk my life for a hit;
completely oblivious to the ultimate cost of my drug of choice.
according to much more experienced dealers,
the drug was free.
i believed them.
trusted them with my life.
was certain they had my best interest in mind.
even as i became more experienced with the drug, i was still deceived by the highs.
they lifted my feet from the ground.
i lost my balance
on the way up
every time.
and when it came time to plant my feet back on the ground
the descent was never easy.
i always came crashing down.
and i would stay there
stretched out, face down
until the opportunity for another hit
became available.
and i'd stretch my arm right back out there.

stick me

truths. and freedom

from the outside, no one could see that i was hurting.
i hid it very well.
it's rather easy when
you drive a mercedes at sixteen,
and take extended vacations in summer.
but what does that really mean
when all you really care about
is love?

i wanted to be loved
in a language that made sense to me.
mama and daddy taught me that love
looked like protection and provision.
i trusted them.
that's why i married the one i did at twenty-two.
we bought a big house with a yard, drove nice cars,
and took extended vacations in summer.

and it still didn't feel like love.

brandie freely

love is touch
and time.
neither of which
was my daddy's language
of love.
so
i let men in
who seemed to want me
badly enough
to touch me.
and spend their time on me.
and
they ended up stealing valuable things
from me.
like touch
and time.

truths. and freedom

and i'm sure that
a different relationship
with you
would've
kept me from losing
so many valuable things.
most notably,
myself.

~~blame~~
-facts

brandie freely

truths. and freedom

i came to better know myself
in college.
i was away from home
away from all the things i thought i knew
away from the things that thought they knew me.
it felt more like reinventing,
rather than finding myself.
i felt at home in college.
that place opened its arms to me.

brandie freely

the longest fall
rewritten pages of my journal ripped to pieces
fall 2003

truths. and freedom

august 25, 2003

i fell in love at first sight of the age-old oak trees whose branches shadow the stone lined pathways.

that slaves once labored these grounds increases my enchantment with this mystical place. even the grass, the greenest i've ever seen, is revered here. there's no walking on the grass. we freshmen are especially careful. the hills in the distance are symbolic of the unkind past that we as a people had to overcome.

a spirit of pride is awakening within me. i don't think i've ever felt as proud to be black. maybe i've never even been so aware of being black.

it feels like i've become a part of an enduring and unyielding legacy. it moves me that i will be educated at the very site where my ancestors were denied this very right. this place. this institution of higher learning will help establish my place in the world. the same world that once held the people i descended from captive to its injustices.

i'm home. and i want nothing more than to add to this rich legacy. what a privilege to be here.

brandie freely

i was an empowered and naïve college freshman
with no grasp of the significance this chapter would play
in the narrative of my life.

if only i could rewind some of those moments
and press the slow motion button.

or if i could whisper to my eighteen year old self,
i'd say:
"slow down young girl.
slow down."

Xx
b

truths. and freedom

but when the possibilities of love are abundant,
it's not always easy to feel your feet on the ground.

brandie freely

An encounter with him was probably inevitable…

Looking back, I wonder how or even if I could have avoided it. We ran in different circles, but had the common passion and love for good music. It fused us together like magnetic energy.

We met at the final rehearsal before I competed in my first college pageant. I was determined to be active and involved in the college life and build up life skills outside of the classroom. I understood that life was just as much about who you know as it was about what you know.

The contestants and I were waiting around to practice our casual wear walk.

"Are you nervous about tomorrow?" Zoe asked me. She was a fellow contestant, and we had enjoyed spending countless nights together preparing for the competition along with twelve others. She was a California girl, and I loved her West Coast persona. She was this pretty little ball of energy, and I was grateful for our blooming friendship.

"A little," I responded. "Mostly about the question and answer segment. Do they have to include that?" We both let out a nervous laugh. "I don't want to make a fool of myself. Or could they at least give us our questions ahead of time, so we can prepare our answers?" I knew the answer to that. Wishful thinking. "Right. I know," she replied. "I'm nervous about that part, too. Being put on the spot in front of hundreds of people is not something I'm looking forward to."

"Neither am I," I looked on. "Other than that, though, I'm more excited than anything," I told her. "This is a really big deal, you know? We're the first ones in our freshmen to be involved with something on this level so far this year. Plus, we're performing in the brand new performing arts hall for the very first time in the University's history. That's kind of amazing!"

I was just about to wonder aloud if that meant we'd be added to the history books when my name was called.

"Brandie, you're up."

I hadn't noticed any additional people in the room, but when my music was cued and Anita Baker's Fairy Tales came on, I heard an unfamiliar voice ask skeptically, "What do you know about Anita Baker?"

My eyebrows furrowed for a second as I glanced to my left to see this audacious individual who'd asked such a question. I got a quick glance of him as I proceeded to practice my walk.

We were required to wear performance heels at each practice. I wonder if it was my walk that took him, or the fact that I appreciated good music. Most of the other contestants had chosen the latest pop and hip-hop to play as they modeled their casual wear.

I'm not sure which it was, but when I turned to walk back, his eyes were glued to me. I came to a stop right in front of him and asked daringly, "What do you know about Anita?" I leaned on to my right leg and placed my hand on my hip.

truths. and freedom

His eyes smiled.

I heard Mrs. Jo, the lead pageant coordinator, laughing in the background, "You haven't heard her sing yet."

His lips parted to say something clever, but I guess words failed him. He just let out a short grunt as his mouth turned up in a grin and he readjusted in his chair.

"Who is that stranger?" Zoe laughed as I gathered my belongings from near her. It was time to rehearse the talent portion of the pageant.

"Girl, I have no idea, but how dare he ask me about Anita?" I was only joking, but she understood how much I loved that soulful voice of hers.

We laughed and headed to meet the rest of the group. During the talent portion everyone found his or her own corners to rehearse in. We would practice on our own until our name was called, then we'd perform for and be critiqued by the coordinators.

I'd chosen to sing a new gospel song by Smokey Norful called I Need You Now. I had rearranged the vocals on the second verse to show off more of my range since it was in a male vocal register. The song was simple, but had a lot of meaning. For some reason everyone fell in love with my rendition, and each night when I'd rehearse it they'd leave their respective corners and sit on the floor right in front of me to listen. It was an amazing feeling that helped me better understand the purpose of my gift.

brandie freely

Tonight was no different. As my name was called to rehearse my song, the other contestants also headed over to the stage area.

I stood there facing them, gripping the mic, and making silly faces to lighten the mood. You could almost touch their anticipation. There room was perfectly still as everyone waited for the music to cue. I was humbled.

As the music cued, I noticed the stranger had stuck around. It made my stomach flutter a little with nervous energy, but by the time I finished singing the first phrase I forgot there was anyone else in the room. My eyes were closed, and I was lost in the moment. When the song ended, I looked down at my peers who were dramatically acting out a black church scene. Fanning, passing out, and shouting. I let out a laugh, "You guys are crazy!"

They continued on as I snuck a peek around the room. There was no sign of him. I quietly asked myself why I even cared.

The night of the pageant was unlike anything I expected. There was standing room only in this sea of black faces. All shades, all sizes, various accents, differing styles of dress. Various personalities: some a little rough around the edges, some almost too refined, and everything you can imagine in between. There were plenty freshmen, some whose faces I knew, but there was also a huge amount of upper classmen doing what my older brother would call 'fishing for fresh meat'.

I tucked my head back into the curtain and rushed back into the dressing room to tell Zoe, "Oh my goodness, Zoe, there are a million people here!" She applied one more layer of lip gloss, pressed her lips together while taking one more glance in the mirror, and then ran out onto the stage with me.
"Look!" I pulled the curtain back slightly.

"Ahhh!" she squealed and then I joined in, too. We couldn't be heard over the roar of the crowd, anyway. We stood there for a moment squeezing each other's hands with nervousness and exhilaration doing a passionate tango in our stomachs.

Back in the dressing room my roommate, Mila, and my mom assisted me with the final touches on my first pageant costume. I was glad my mom was there. If I were performing in front of the President of The United States of America, plus the Pope, and Anita Baker, I'd be confident so long as she was also in attendance. My mama was always my biggest fan, the greatest supporter of my life, my one sure thing.

Without warning, loud base and vibrations came seeping through the walls. I looked around and most of the freshmen had confused looks like me. "Where is that coming from?" was being whispered throughout the room.

The upperclassmen, however, who were there to assist backstage had different reactions altogether.

An almost aggressive excitement came over them as they moved to the beat and looked at one another with knowing eyes.

"The DJ is here!" one of them said. "Let's go!"

A group of them ran off, but not before letting us all know that they'd, "Be right back!"

"You're not leaving me, I wanna see!" one of the contestants said as she hurried behind them.
We all decided to go and see what the hoopla was about. We took turns peeking through the curtain to witness the commotion for ourselves.

When it was my turn, the first thing I noticed was how the crowd was reacting to the music. Mostly everyone was out of their seat dancing and having a great time! I saw girls with major rhythm moving their bodies seductively in the aisles and all over the auditorium. Guys were nodding their heads and standing up to get a better view of the girls. I was captivated by the scene. I almost envied their boldness, because I loved to dance. I loved to move my body as an outward expression of how music made me feel inside. I just never quite found the courage to do it in front of others. I was afraid of being judged. I decided right then that I wanted to change that. I wanted to be free to have as much fun as they appeared to be having.

The next thing I noticed was the DJ. He was wearing a red baseball cap and a white graphic tee with black wording. His head was down, and one hand was gripping his headphones. The other hand was moving madly on the keyboard of his laptop. He was focused on the screen, though his head was bobbing wildly to the beat. He was mixing some old school favorites of mine like, Frankie Beverly and Maze with some 90's R&B like Jodeci. Then he'd throw in some current rap artists, then top it with 80's hip hop. When MJ's "rock with you" started to play, the crowd lost it! You could almost hear a simultaneous, "That's my jam!" echo through the room.

I'd never been in an atmosphere like this. Each time he switched to a different hit, the crowd would go absolutely crazy again. It was awesome! I was a bit surprised at how the energy level fueled me. I was getting more and more excited about how the night was going to unfold.

Just as I started to pull my head back in the curtain, the DJ looked up. It was him. I immediately recognized that grin and those smiling eyes. I watched him for another moment and then thought: So, that's why you were intrigued by my taste in music...
I smirked and pulled my head back in.

The pageant was ah-mazing.

My casual wear, a denim suit with a striped button down dress shirt underneath was a hit. It was the first look for each contestant, and our official pageant introduction. I walked out to the beat of my favorite Anita song, confident and having the time of my life. I smiled so hard, I could feel my mouth trembling and hoped the onlookers wouldn't notice. The audience approved.

My biggest feat, though, was winning over the crowd with my voice. I'd been told that if the crowd didn't like your talent, you'd know it. I'd heard horror stories of performers, professional ones, even celebrities who'd been paid to perform at homecoming and other campus events, who had been booed off stage by the students here. This university boasted of a tough crowd.

I approached the mic and grabbed it. The cord was hanging loosely, so I wrapped it around my right hand as I grabbed the mic with my left. I adjusted it to my mouth before looking out into the crowd to take in the moment.

I met several eyes as I scanned the room. Most were looking at me, and saying something to their neighbor at the same time. My mom sat up front and to my left. Mila was there and gave me a last minute smile as the music cued.

The hushed conversations continued throughout the room even as the music intro played. I took a deep breath and sang the first phrase. In the pause between it and the next phrase, there was complete silence except for a singular yell of approval from somewhere in the balcony. I silently thanked them as my eyes closed, so that I could open up and sing from my heart. I didn't get booed off. It was actually quite the opposite.

truths. and freedom

I took home the crown that night. What a high.

The room's mainline rang. I moved from a comfortable position on my bed to answer it.

"Hello?"

"Brandie, you have a visitor at the front."

"Okay, thanks. Be there in a minute." I hung up and slid on my flip-flops.

Walking toward the front desk I spoke to a few of my building mates who were hanging out in the hallway or in the lounge area. As I passed by, some yelled out their congratulations on winning the pageant. I was still soaking in the whole thing.

"Thanks, girl!" I said to Tay who was sitting in her room with the door opened. She was from Dallas, and we'd become quick friends during Panther Camp, which was the week-long orientation for first year students. There were so many cool and relatable people in our freshman class, and especially in my building; 37. I felt blessed to share such a rich experience with so many amazing people; we were family.

As I turned the corner to approach the front desk, I didn't see anyone. I stuck my head in the window of the reception area.

"Emma?" I called for the student worker who recorded the visitors who came to our building.

She came out from the back conference room wearing a sorority shirt and torn jeans. Extremely pretty and sweet, she smiled and pointed toward the glass entrance to our building. "He's out there."

I wondered who 'he' was and looked anxiously through the glass to find out. Since the pageant, there had been plenty of guys who were interested in spending time with me, but none had been so bold as to show up uninvited to my building. Who in the world? I asked myself.

There, sitting on a concrete stoop that lead to an emergency exit from our neighboring building sat the DJ, the stranger, the guy with smiling eyes. I felt a slight flutter in my stomach and didn't know why.

"Thanks Emma," I said as I walked to the door and pushed it open.

When he heard the door, he looked up. The brim of his blue baseball cap sort of hid his face. He stood to greet me, but before he could say anything I said, "It's cool. We can sit here." I don't know what made me feel we should sit. Why had I even suggested that?

He replied through a slight smile, "Cool." I tried, but failed not to smile back.

We sat.

"You did awesome in the pageant. Congrats on being crowned Miss U. College."

"Why thank you," I said too kindly and gave him a playful push on the arm. He leaned way over as if I'd pushed harder than I did and then came back towards me with a playful grin. I looked at him for a moment too long, and his smiling eyes became serious.

He had profound brown eyes. They were big, which made him seemingly innocent. Yet they were demanding and intense. They stared back at me and I nearly melted right on that concrete stoop. We both looked away to compose ourselves.

"Congrats to you," I broke the silence.

His expression became puzzled. "For what?"

"For being so awesome that night." My words were sincere. "The way you got the crowd moving and out of their seats. I loved it. I think they had the most fun before the show started and during the intermissions."

We both let out a chuckle.

"Ha. Yeah. Thanks." He looked into the distance. "Awesome, huh?"

"Yeah, I thought the energy was amazing. I've honestly never seen anything like it."

He looked at me. "What do you mean?"

"I just mean I've never really been around loud music and people moving that way. That's all."

I knew my response sounded ridiculous and was prepared for him to say something about me being sheltered or needing to live a little, or something to that effect. It was the same response I always got from people when they learned of my inexperience in clubs, parties, etc. I knew nothing about that life, and honestly had never been interested in it.

"I figured as much."

Squinting my eyes, I looked at him. Our eyes met for a moment, before we both nervously looked away.

"You figured what?" I wanted to know.

He looked at me again, his eyes a lighter brown than I'd first thought. The setting sun illuminated their depth. "I figured you were a good girl."
I laughed a little too loud, "A good girl? I never said all that." I tried to sell him a naughty girl grin, but he didn't buy in. His eyes smiled at me instead.

"You are a good girl." he was almost laughing. "It's okay!"

He was staring at me now, and I was captivated. I wanted him to say more. I wanted to ask him how he knew, what'd made him feel that way about me.

As if he'd read my mind he said, "There's something special about you. I watched you in rehearsal, how you encouraged the others. You were selflessly concerned about everyone's experience. You wanted it to be good for everybody. I was intrigued by your taste in music. You must not care about what's popular. I think that's special and rare. And I witnessed how the others gravitated to you like metal to a magnet. I felt that same energy then, and I feel it now."

When his voice stopped, I remembered to breathe.

I took in a deep breath, and not having enough time to gather myself to say something clever, replied, "Wow. Well, I guess maybe it's not such a bad thing, then? To be a good girl. I mean, clearly you're a good guy. You came all the way across campus to return my music." I reached for the cd he was holding with my name on it. "Did you hand deliver everyone's cd's?

His left eyebrow twitched. "Nah." he let out a nervous laugh and found a stick to play with on the concrete beneath us.

I didn't know what to say, so I found something to stare at atop the building. My eyes settled on a brick. I studied it, wondering how many individual bricks it took to cover the entire building.

"I'm a bad guy."

"You're a bad guy?!" My eyes pleaded when they met his. I reached for him, and in a friendly but firm manner grabbed his wrist. "You're not a bad guy."

I didn't know the person sitting next to me. I had no

idea whether he was a bad guy or not, but his words tugged at my heart. I didn't like his undertone. It was then that I noticed a hint of sadness in those brown eyes. Maybe not sadness, but some kind of heaviness, and I didn't like it. We stared at one another for a moment. I studied him trying to figure out what it was and knowing that whatever it was I wanted it gone.

We sat on that stoop until it was completely dark out. Shadows could be seen moving around through the windows of my building. We laughed, taking turns guessing what the people might be doing in their rooms. Some shadows moved back and forth, back and forth. I wouldn't have even noticed the people going in and out of the building were it not for the occasional short pauses in our conversation. We talked about our origins and families. He was raised by his mother. Her only child. Her golden child. He'd attended private schools and was an award winning writer. I was impressed. I shared my interests with him. We had a lot of common interests. Art and literature and poetry and music. And lyricism. We both loved words. The art of language.

As I told him more about me, he listened intently as if everything I said was particularly important. He listened as I told him about growing up as a pastor's daughter. We talked about religion. He believed in God, but felt convicted by some of the decisions he'd made in his life.

The look I didn't like returned to his eyes.

I leaned into him, "You're not a bad guy."
He looked into my eyes as if searching for the truth.
And he found it there.

We both smiled.

When I returned to my room it was late. Mila was still up. Her television adding a glow to the dark room. Martin re-runs were playing. Our absolute favorite.

She looked up from painting her nails. Her eyes glared at me over her frames, and then squinted. "Hey," she said slowly. Knowingly. Inquisitively.

I smiled and gave her a side eye. "Hey."

She sat up abruptly and said, "Spill!"

I plopped down on her bed and released a heavy breath. Had I breathed much at all while he and I spoke? I couldn't remember. I crossed my legs together in front of me and then leaned over until my chin rested in my hands.

Words failed me, and Mila was impatient, "What? What happened? What'd he want?" she probed.

"Wait. How'd you know it was him?"

"I'm still waiting to learn who 'he' is, but I saw you outside when I went down the hall to visit Patty for a while. She burned some music onto a CD for us."

"Sweet!" I said and sat up. Pattie was another building mate. She was super generous and had an eclectic taste in music. We'd go visit her for new sounds. She was more than happy to burn copies for us from her computer. All we had to do was provide the blank CDs.

"So, who is he?" she stressed refusing to allow the subject to change.

I looked at her, looked away, and then bit my lip to keep my mouth from turning up into a ridiculous grin. I drew in a deep breath and then spilled, "He's the DJ. He's the guy from rehearsal that I mentioned to you who asked me about Anita Baker. His name is Cole."

Mila leaned in nodding her head slowly, but her eyebrows were furrowed. "Uh huh…" it was more of a question than a response.

"And he stopped by to return my cd from the pageant."

"Right," she retorted. "And it took all these hours to accomplish that task?"

All at once my thoughts escaped me and came spilling from my mouth. "Okay. Okay. So he… is… um… really cool? And we actually have a lot in common. I don't know, I guess I kind of felt something between us even that day at rehearsal, but I never really paid any mind to what it might be, because I didn't know much about him, or if I'd see him again. Besides, you know I'm trying to focus on school and I have Dane to consider." (Dane was my long distance boyfriend.) "I just don't want to forget what's important. I didn't come to college to fall in love. I came to get a degree, and that's where my energy needs to be. You know what I'm saying?"

I expected the perplexed look she was giving me when our eyes met.

"Wait, what? Fall in love?" She readjusted her legs under her and moved her locs from her face slowly so as not to mess up her nails. "Brandie" she laughed lightly. "Slow down."

I let out a knowing chuckle. "Look. He was just super cool, you know? We talked about a lot of things, and I just enjoyed our conversation. I liked the ease of our exchange. And the substance of it. The interest level. We talked about things that actually mattered, you know?" I looked to see if she was getting it, and she was. "There was no small talk involved, and I liked that. I liked him. I like him. That's all."

"Well, there's no harm in that, right? He seems like an interesting enough guy. You don't have to fall in love with him." She stretched out love. "It's possible to just be friends with a guy. Don't you think?"

I was silent for a moment considering the appropriate answer to that question. My mind said no. It's not possible. But then I remembered the trace of sadness in his eyes. Maybe all he needed was a friend. I mean self-control wouldn't be a problem as long as I kept my priorities in order. Right?

"Yeah. I mean, I think it's possible. Anything is

possible," I said to convince her and me. I stood to head over to the restroom. I needed to shower and sleep, so I could be at my 8:00 class on time in the morning.

Just friends seemed really nice, actually. And refreshing, I thought to myself.

My phone rang at 1:17 am. Over the past few days I'd become familiar with the number on the screen.

My stomach fluttered delightfully.

I pushed talk on my phone, "Hi," I spoke low so as not to disturb Mila.

"Hi." he said back. "Ready?"

"I am."

I hung up the phone and crawled out of bed. I unwrapped my hair and finger combed through it, then slipped into my favorite pair of jeans. I slid on a nearby pair of converse and grabbed my keys and phone as smoothly as possible.

Just as I was tiptoeing through the door, Mila readjusted in bed and said, "Have fun and be safe."

I smiled in the darkness and replied, "Sure thing."

I'd been looking forward to seeing Cole again. We'd

truths. and freedom

spoken briefly on a few occasions, but were always pressed for time due to completely different schedules. He was busy between classes and gigging. I was also busy juggling classes and my new duties as Miss U. College. I was often asked to speak and sing at events around campus, and I was also building a new student organization alongside Mr. U College. We were calling it The Self-Empowerment Association. We had several events already in the works, and I was both excited and overwhelmed by college life.

It was different from what I expected, but in a great way. I loved meeting new people and learning the ins and outs of organizing, networking, and time-management. I hadn't realized how much of my education would actually occur outside of the classroom. The experience was invaluable. I learned how creative I was. How many ideas I had that were actually good. What an effective leader I was; how people gravitated toward me and listened when I spoke. I definitely found my voice in college.

I walked out the glass doors of our building and looked to my right towards the street. He was leaning on the driver's door of a champagne Chrysler. His legs remained crossed and arms folded as I walked towards him. I had this really good feeling. Like stepping out of a steaming hot shower into the coolness. He was a breath of fresh air.

His eyes smiled at me when we were close enough to see each other clearly. He walked away from me, and I almost paused until I realized he was walking around to open the passenger door. My smile grew from the inside.

It was going to be a great ride.

When we were both inside he leaned back, looked over at me, and stared. He said nothing verbally, but everything with his eyes. I couldn't help but look away for a moment. His eyes pierced right through me. Could he hear my thoughts? I wondered.

I found an object to focus on through the window. I needed to gather myself. We were to be friends. That was it. That was all. There were to be no feelings attached here. Focus Brandie.

When I turned back, his gaze was still there. His mouth turned up into a smirk, "You good?"

I couldn't not smile when I replied, "I'm good." He can see my thoughts, I laughed to myself.
"What's funny?" he wanted to know as he finally put the car into drive and pulled off.

"Nothing at all," I replied sarcastically. "Just drive your car, Mister."

He chuckled and said, "Yes ma'am. What about the air? Is it okay?"

"It's a little cold," I said. "I'm super cold all the time."
"Not a problem," he said as he casually reached over to adjust the temperature.

While he was messing with the dash he slightly

increased the music volume on the radio. I recognized the song and naturally began humming along to it.

He looked over at me with a surprised look, but grinning. "You know this song?"

"Oh my goodness, yes! I like, loooove Dwele! Are you kidding?!"

"That's crazy! I love this dude's music, too, but not too many people know about him."

"I know, but isn't that the best, though? I secretly don't want my favorites to get too much fame and notoriety. I wanna keep 'em to myself, you know what I'm saying? I mean, typically when artists get main stream success, their musical style changes. Right? What do you think?"

"No, I totally agree. Underground artists are always the purest. They're hungrier, too."

"Exactly. I mean, in my opinion, a lot of my favorite artists deserve Grammy's for their work, but they'll probably never get one. And if they do I'm not sure they'll remain my favorites for long. How many artists have changed their styles over the course and successes of their careers?"

He started to list off various singers and hip hop artists that he'd lost respect for. Most of them were on my list, too. We were so deep into our conversation that I forgot to ask where we were going. We'd been riding for a while by then.

"Cole, where're we headed?"

"Somewhere we can talk," he said. Just ride."
I relaxed in my seat enjoying the vibes that filled the car. I sang quietly to Dwele as he bobbed his head coolly and drove to our destination. Before long we were coming up on city lights and nightlife. I recognized the area. Houston. I was from a city not too far east of here. He exited Westheimer and made a right. I'd never been in the area at this time of night and was rapt by its magnificence. Lights trimmed the trees, though it wasn't yet Christmas time. Young, eclectic people were seated outside at bistros having what I assumed were intellectual conversations about art and love. I was inspired.

I heard the blinker come on and looked to see where we were turning. To the right of us was the largest Starbucks I'd ever seen, and sure enough, it would be the location of tonight's conversation. He pulled into the drive thru, since the inside was closed.

"What would you like?" he asked.

I'd never ordered a specialty coffee before and had no clue. "Um? I don't really know. Anything sweet, really. What should I get?" He saw the helpless look on my face.

"Don't worry about it. Sit back, I got you."

We pulled up to the window and he ordered two Caramel Macchiatos. "You want anything else?" he asked.

truths. and freedom

"Uhh? No, that's fine. Thanks, though." I smiled at him.

"It's my pleasure," he smiled back.

We pulled back around and parked the car next to the building. "Come on," he said.

I got out and followed him to a sitting area outside the building that offered an unobstructed view of the stunning city lights. We found a table and sat. He placed a black notebook and our drinks on the table before sitting across from me.

Our conversation was effortless. At nineteen years old, I was finally speaking a language that made perfect sense to me. Like it was my native tongue. Like I was home. I understood every word he spoke and every space in between.

Without explanation or introduction he opened his notebook and read a piece to me entitled 'Horrible Man". I listened intently to the passion and sincerity in his voice. I was moved.

"Are those your words?"

"Yes," his brown eyes were glowing under the streetlights.

That was the moment my feet no longer felt the ground, and there was no slowing down on my way up. I'd never been high like this before.

From that night, our time together was filled with no

less passion. Every word shared was lyrical and every look struck a chord that would echo endlessly.

Spontaneous rides to nowhere just before dawn were our norm. Conversation was never a necessity on those back roads. We spoke with our eyes or his hands running through my hair. His fingers dancing along my thigh was evidence enough that he got a kick out of me. I was his muse and he was mine. I'd never been inspired by love before.

truths. and freedom

October 25, 2003
3:30 am

I can't believe tonight.
We shared our first kiss.
Setting: winding road, sunset.

I say to him, "Stop the car."

"What do you mean? I can't stop the car right now; we're in the middle of the road," he wears confusion and intrigue on his face.

"Just stop the car." I look around, heart pounding, "There are no cars behind us."

He comes to a stop, puts the car in park and looks over at me. I move in closer, the corners of my mouth turned up into a manipulative grin. I take his mouth, and he receives mine. The kiss is long and deep. Right there in the middle of the road that led to the university I'd fallen in love with at first sight. A paved road underneath the stars and those age-old trees.

I felt my body responding in a way it never has before. If I'm being honest, I'm a little scared, because if it heats into a flame, I'm sure the fire will be hard to extinguish.

Xx
b

brandie freely

truths. and freedom

and that is how and where my heart got stuck.
somewhere on one of those winding roads in the dark.
abandoned.
at a crossroad
where i wanted to go right
and his internal navigation was pulling him left.

i waited in the dark for him to return.
even as others passed by and tried to rescue me.

i felt that magnetic pull
no matter how far away he was.

and when he'd come back my way
it took nothing to reignite a
spark that never, ever quite
died.
we'd try to go the same way again
back down another dark winding road.
until we came right back to the very
same
damned
crossroad.

as the fall lingered on
and the leaves dried up
and floated to
the ground
i
waited still.
made a pile
to rest on while
i watched for him
through the darkness.
until eventually there was a light
that caused me to sit up

the glow grew
as it neared.

i stood.
squinted my eyes
to see.

fire.

the end was near.

truths. and freedom

and when that dreaded time came
i raced wildly towards the raging flames.
my tears like waterfalls
misting in the wind

i was ravaged
but resilient

as i neared the blaze
i felt the heat
of a fire that spewed debris and black smoke
relentlessly towards me

and i could hardly breathe.
could hardly see.
but still i ran
towards a fire
escalating uncontrollably

a fire i had to stop
before it
ruined
everything in my path.

i ran and cried
ran and cried
ignoring the pang of fear in my chest

i knew you had to be extinguished
before you destroyed me

i knew
danger was imminent
burns inevitable

and that there was sure to be scars.
but i was ready to use logic
in the fight
to save myself.
from the
truth

about
love.

truths. and freedom

love vs. logic
was the battle
of her life
and her greatest opponent
was time.

brandie freely

truths. and freedom

and so
i found refuge in someone
just like my
father
so that
i
wouldn't
get
burned.

again.

-logic

brandie freely

i should've walked away from the very start.
i didn't because
he was different
from those who'd hurt me before.
so i figured maybe he wouldn't hurt me
and i was right.
he would do everything perfectly
and i'd have no reason
to say no
when he
asked me
to be his wife.

and i'd say yes,
because
no
isn't
really
a
thought
when
all you have to believe in
are the fixed ideas of your youth
that you
never reconsidered
as an adult.

truths. and freedom

so.
i exchanged vows
i didn't mean
or wholly understand.
i made promises that
i would break.
i remember feeling nothing.
except the ridges being carved into my rib cage by
the wires in my wedding dress.
i remember
wanting to get out of that dress.
i remember having no desire to consummate our
marriage that night.

i wanted out of the dress.
that was digging into me
holding me in like a cage.

i wanted it off,
but not with his help
because i didn't
want to give him reason
to touch me or to be that close.
i remember telling myself i was just tired
and that the honeymoon would be different.

i remember it wasn't.

so i had someone else
free me
from the wires inside
the dress i'd chosen to step into
on the very first day i went dress shopping.
i remember i didn't put much thought

brandie freely

into it.
it was exactly my size.
it was discounted, since it was a sample dress.
it seemed meant to be.
seemed.
meant.
but during the course of my wedding day
it felt heavy.
and i
felt heavier.

truths. and freedom

i understood your vision for us.
knew your desires very well.
sincerely thought mine matched,
but quickly realized they didn't.
i guess i'm the type of person
who learns from experience.
and i'm sorry that
our experience
taught me all about a life
i didn't want.

three months in
you went in the attic
and found
a journal
that held my past
in colorful detail.
you used those details to paint me a different shade,
and neither of us ever returned to our original hue
after that.
did we?

we were darker.
blended with the colors you found in the details.
blended with the colors we were before there was a
we.
we didn't see each other the same after that.
did we?
yet in the end when
all the colors would fade to black
you would pretend
that you never saw anything at all.

as if i'd changed on my own.

you knew the truth.
didn't you?

truths. and freedom

four years
is a long time.
especially when time
doesn't seem to be on your side.
and when
predictability makes life move slowly.

there was no
spontaneity
between us.
everything was calculated,
literally.
apparently we couldn't afford
joy.
and
excitement was too expensive.
so we
went without
in an effort to save up
for a tomorrow that
would
never.
come.

but i didn't want to hurt you
so i kept staying
a little longer
every time one foot
was out the door.

truths. and freedom

i resented the life i'd chosen for myself.
regretted my decision to walk
into a cage.

i wanted to be free.

none of it really had anything to do with you.
i was twenty-two.
i was only beginning to discover who
i really was.
i didn't really know what i was doing.
and i was still learning about what i wanted.
unfortunately, i'd never thought too deeply about it
before.

but i knew this wasn't it.

i just didn't know how to
undo
the things i'd made you believe.

i had believed those things, too.

we both thought i was someone i wasn't.

i was the great pretender.
and there would be a price to pay.
if i wanted to stop pretending.

that i loved playing the role
of your happy wife
in this beautiful house
only
a few doors down

brandie freely

from parents who were proud of me
for doing the right thing.
and
a church
and community
who were proud that
someone
had gotten it right.

truths. and freedom

i just didn't want to be boxed in.
and it's not that you boxed me in.
i boxed me in.
i failed to imagine more.
failed to color outside
my own lines.
i failed
to consider becoming something more
than
just
someone's
woman.
i wish i'd considered
belonging to myself.
first.

brandie freely

i didn't know me,
so it was impossible for you to.

truths. and freedom

finally, the end came.
as no surprise
to either of us.
years of hoping and pretending
that things could be different.
going to therapy just to admit
in front of a non biased stranger
that i wasn't in love with you.
thinking that would
be enough to make you walk away
so i wouldn't have to.

there were times i wished
the therapist would
break the confidentiality
of our one on one sessions
and tell you
that i was still in love
with a guy
i'd met in college.

that i never stopped loving him
or wanting him.
and that he
was still
in and out
of my dreams
and

he was still in and out of
my life.

brandie freely

truths. and freedom

he called the week before my wedding:

"i heard you were getting married sooner than later."

i confirm.
silence.
deep breaths.

would he tell me?
tell me not to do it, because we were meant.
would he save me from this mistake?
say it.
please.
tell me.

deeper breaths.

"i know you wanted it to be me."

i confirm again. this time with silence.

my eyes and ears are burning.
say it.
my heart is burning.
say it.
i need you to.
save me.

more silence

as my cheeks
soak up
my tears.
but even if you had said it

what could i have done?
i wasn't brave enough
or heartless enough
to leave one for another.
that would be the most unrighteous
unfair
and selfish
thing i could ever do.
and
i would rather
the suffering from one bad decision
than the karma
of another.

truths. and freedom

truth is:
we never loved each other at the same time.
you and i.
either you were all in, and i wasn't.
or i was all in, and you weren't.
time was never on our side.
or maybe it was.
maybe we wanted something
that was just never meant to be.
maybe we were
just a like all the other
tragic
love stories.
a tragic inevitability.

i remember the first time you reached out
several months after the wedding.
it was summer.
i didn't answer your call.
didn't want to do the wrong thing.
at first.
until
one day i randomly checked my old email.
in it,
i found a note from you asking me to please
call.
said you were on a road trip
and were listening
to dwele, our favorite.
the last line asked once more
call me. please.

and i did.
not because i thought i loved you still,
but because i swore i didn't.
anymore.

phone calls turned into meet ups.
just like that.
turns out i did
still love you

meet ups turned into talks of what ifs.
just like that.

confessions of unhappiness.
confessions of uncertainties.
confessions of a love that didn't die just because
i'd married someone else
just like that.

truths. and freedom

our affair wasn't consistent.
nothing about it was predictable.
it was more like a wondrous escapism.
a natural adventure,
which is something i was missing at home.
at home he insisted on over analyzing budgets and
mapping out plans
for every. single. thing.
that didn't feel like living to me.
i wasn't fond of it.
but
i was fond of your random, poetic texts
that cajoled me to spend a day with you
even after not hearing from you for months.
my heart would race,
and it would feel amazing
to feel
anything
at
all.
so
i'd go
sometimes.
and spend time
feeling alive.
even if only for a while.

brandie freely

i remember you'd kiss only the tips
of my fingers
one by one
and somehow
the tingle stopped only
when it reached the nape of my neck
just where the fine hair fed into the mass of wildness
which
his hand somehow
knew its way through.

truths. and freedom

it was easy to pretend
nothing was going on
outside of home
because i'd been
pretending
that something was going on
inside of home
seamlessly.

and one day it happened.
the unspeakable.
as horrible as the act was
it was familiar for us.
it wouldn't be the first relationship
sabotaged by our carelessness
the only
difference this time
was that i was wearing
a beautiful two karat solitaire diamond ring.

i was overcome with emotion as soon as you entered me.
i cried.
i did.

but i didn't let you see.
i hid
from you and from shame
there
in my exposed skin.

truths. and freedom

i'm sure the most ideal
time
to tell you
was when
i found out i was pregnant
and you asked me
if there was a chance
that she
was not yours.
you knew
i'd been with
the guy from the pages
in my journal
that you ripped apart.
you knew
because i told you.
because you saw the mud on the back, passenger
wheel of my truck that night.
and i couldn't lie
then
like was i able to when
i told you
there was no chance
she wasn't yours.
i couldn't
look you in the eyes and tell the truth
because
i wasn't brave enough.
i wasn't bold enough
to admit
that i had done something so wrong.
i was afraid
of being that flawed of a human.
i couldn't even accept

truths. and freedom

the truth for myself.
how would i convince you to?
you didn't want my truth, either.

i lied because:

one:
the realism of what was happening was far too much to bear.

two:
i didn't even know how to begin a sentence with the words that needed to be said.

three:
the life i had was good the way it was, and i could just keep it all up.
we were picture perfect, and no one would ever look close enough to see this one flaw.

four:
i could not be held responsible for breaking someone's heart in this manner.
i just couldn't.

five:
i actually prayed that a miracle might happen, and the truth would somehow cease to exist.

six:
i was used to pretending anyway.

seven:
it would be okay. it would.

eight:
i hadn't intended on this happening. i didn't mean for it to happen.

truths. and freedom

i hadn't done this on purpose. and god knew that.

nine:
i was keeping the baby that was growing inside of me.
i wanted her.
always had.

and even as time and life
went on
as though nothing was the matter.
the truth sat still on my shoulder
never saying a word
just there.
sitting.
like a fact.
unchangeable
by events, people, things, feelings, emotion, places,
times, circumstances, ideas, opinions, beliefs,
relationships, codes, rules, worlds, rulers, science,
space, or anything else.

it remained.

truths. and freedom

i thought i was doing the best thing for my daughter.
i believed a stable life was the best thing for her.
it was what i had. it was all i knew.
and it was what i considered to be right.
i wanted to do right by her.
wanted to provide her with the things i had
so she'd have a chance of turning out okay.
like i had.
you know?

but even as i'd go throughout the day
going through all sorts of motions
and pretending

the truth would sit.
i'd see it on my shoulder when i looked into the mirror.

it wouldn't say anything,
but
i'd see it.
and it saw me.
and we'd stare into one another
searching.

for freedom.

brandie freely

truths. and freedom.

my mother is the one who introduced me to the phrase "beauty flows from a heart that's free".
i have coined it as one of my personal truths.

i had an affair on sporadic dates and episodes throughout my four year marriage. it was never consistent. it was more of a random escapism. it was not with a random person. it was instead with a person i'd loved since my freshman year in college, which was 4 years prior to my marriage. i even knew i still loved him, and got married anyway. why? "if i'm being honest, i chose security over risk. plain and simple.

anyway, one of those episodes led to the conception of my daughter.

i did not immediately reveal this truth to my then husband. i instead carried the secret around, only sharing it with three others. for over a year, i kept it from my friends, family, and most horribly the man who was unknowingly raising her as his own. i was in a mental hell the entire time. it was a spiritual warfare like nothing i've ever experienced. i would wish the turmoil on no one.

in 2011, after (i repeat after) a mutual decision with my then husband to separate for unrelated issues, i decided that i needed to tell the truth. once i exposed myself my world all but fell apart. for the next year i would face some of the most trying experiences of my life. the agony i felt because of the hurt i'd caused others. the shame that took over my conscious. facing my parents, my dad's church, my brothers, and my mother. knowing that i looked like an adulterous and deceitful woman, and not wanting to have that label for the rest of my life. not knowing if a man would ever love me because i was impure. it was agonizing.

truths. and freedom

there was this one thing, though. inside, aside from worrying about what others thought of me, i felt ah-mazing. i can't describe the feeling, other than that it was absolutely liberating. i no longer felt burdened down. i was un-caged. i felt that the weight of the world had been lifted from my shoulders. i couldn't explain it at first, but eventually i recognized that the truth had set me free. that phrase became so real to me.

it goes without saying that it was a costly truth, but i think that my life now illustrates how priceless it also was.

people who refuse to confess truths will continue to have to cover-up or 'put on' to impress people. these individuals will find it difficult to see the glass as half full. they will not appreciate the simplicities of life, because their life is far too complicated. their vision is blurred with pessimism. they'll have to search incessantly for fulfillment because they are subconsciously searching for the truth. free people don't have these issues. the truth, i have found, makes you feel whole. truth is being self aware and unashamed of having flaws. it's a far better way to live than to pretend you have things together all the time. how exhausting?!

maybe some people are never told it's okay to be imperfect. somewhere along the way, maybe they were told that they weren't good enough. maybe they took those words and established their lives around it. they will quite possibly die never having explored who they truly are.

where do we lose ourselves along the way? we must go back and rediscover who we were made to be.

maybe you're currently asking yourself what are your big flaws or secrets, and you're like i don't really have any.

we all are flawed. what makes us free and beautiful is when we are earnest and meek enough to acknowledge it. maybe not in a book or to the whole world, but maybe just to ourselves. open confession is good for the soul. and moreover, it brings on healing. once we are healed, we are whole again. once we are whole, we desire to help someone else get to that place.

i used to look in the mirror and abhor what was staring back at me. through open confession, and fearlessness to face whatever the end result would be, i can now say that i love exactly who i am flaws and all.

take it from me, there's no feeling like being free.

and you'll be surprised at the people who want to be around you, just so they can get a little piece of freedom and what looks to them like pure happiness. they open up to you about their skeletons, because it's held them captive for too long. they've wanted to open up, but never felt safe enough to do it. it feels great being that safe haven. they trust you, because they know you have no room to judge.

truths. and freedom

i have no room to judge. who really does?

just think. what if we all opened up, confessed and revealed our true selves? think of how safe and commonplace this world would be... how non-judgmental...
don't die as someone else. take this opportunity, this life, to live freely as exactly who you are supposed to be.

i think you'll find it's worth it...

brandie freely

truths. and freedom

solona

my daughter. the one who made me brave.

i came alive.

one day she'll ask, and i'll tell her to close her eyes while i tell her the most beautiful love story. she'll want to know every detail, and i will relay them to her in a way that paints a perfect portrait of a woman who comes alive with every stroke of the master artist's brush.

she'll understand her role in bringing the story to life.

"close your eyes now baby, you are my reason. let me explain how."

i wasn't expecting you to show up the way you did.

you are my most beautiful surprise.

still frames.

there is a still frame in my memory of the first time i saw my daughter. she was as perfect. the doctor lifted her and placed her on my bare chest, skin to skin, just as we'd discussed. her faint cry was honestly the sweetest sound i had ever heard. i began to speak calmly to her, and this brand new little human opened her eyes and tried to lift her head to see her mommy. i tilted my head so that we could see one another for the very first time. "oh there you are," i spoke to her. she was mine, and i was hers.

no one else mattered anymore in that moment. truth be told, i felt very possessive of her. i felt that she was only mine. i was the only one who really **knew** her. i held in my arms a tangible secret.

i might have kept the secret had it not meant that she may never know her own self…

but as long as i am able, i will always do what is in her best interest. she deserved and deserves to know exactly who she is.

that is **the** reason i came clean about my infidelity. i could have gone on maybe forever lying to others, but my darling girl? she deserves the best from her mother. whatever my best might be. and i am much better than a liar.

were there benefits to coming clean for me? absolutely.

truth is the thing that set me free.

love child.

before i was ever married, i had this kind of secret dream that i shared with my closest friends. i only said it when we were talking freely, almost joking about our futures. and we were usually doing a little male bashing if i mentioned it.

i would say, "you know what? i just wanna travel the world. all i need is a little love child to come along for the adventure."

they would laugh with me as i joked about not having to have a man in the equation.

i'd say, "listen. he can just give me my perfect little side kick, and i'm good. we'll be off to see the world. just us two." i could see the whole thing so vividly. i even had a mental picture of what he or she would look like. –not kidding!

–looked a lot like my daughter, truth be told.

i just felt like maybe that's what was written for me. i'm not sure why. but i was very open to the possibility.

when i got pregnant with my daughter, i guess you could say the possibility became very real. after her first birthday, i was sure it was going to happen.

it was going to be just the two of us. my love child and i –yes, she is a love child.

it was during that time that i learned what it felt like to

truths. and freedom

only depend on me.

it was hard because of the circumstances, but it was worth it because of the growth i experienced. i got really acquainted with myself.

in so many ways, the situation made me better.

i'm sure that's true for any mom. for me, it's more than just the responsibilities that we're required to take on.

it's more than practicing the art of balance, it's even more than learning to put someone's needs before our own sometimes.

for me, it's the idea that my daughter is a tangible piece of god's grace.

i believe he gave her to me so that i could plainly see his love for me.

brandie freely

experience.

a collection of still relevant essays from my twenties.

good intentions.

perhaps the most valuable lesson i've learned in the past two to three years is this: when it comes to people, "good intentions" mean very little (if anything at all).

what i mean is that you could have the absolute best intentions concerning someone, but all that will matter in the end are the effects of your acts and deeds.

there was a time that i truly thought my good intentions were enough to cover my faults. i grew up hearing the phrase 'god knows your heart'. i had never considered that the phrase excluded people. people didn't know my heart, and in most cases weren't concerned about it. i think, though, that i thought those closest to me would know me well enough to know that i am a person of 'good intention'. i don't set out to hurt people. i am not like that. surely they knew that. so i thought...

these people. i mean, they had even said it to me. "brandie, you are truly a special somebody. your compassion can be felt. your heart is big. you truly love people", etc. they'd witnessed me in conflicts and knew that i didn't have a malicious bone in my body. i'd shared my ideals with these people. they admired me for those ideals and morals.

how then, could they be so quick to forget?

i remember sitting at this long table for a first attempt

at mediation in my divorce. the court reporter was at
the head of the table, to the right of me. my attorney
was in between us. across from me: the most unkempt
guy i'd ever seen. tall with sloppy, ill-fitting clothes,
and just not together; he was the other attorney in the
case. next to him sat my soon to be ex-husband.

the look on his face was one of disgust mixed with 'i
don't want her to see how bad this hurts inside'. things
got real for me that day, because every word that
escaped the mouths of the two men across from me
painted this picture of some woman who was not me.
the woman they were describing was a heart-breaker.

she was heartless. she was conniving, manipulative,
and untrue. they weren't describing me. i was none of
those things. i thought that people knew that about
me. people knew that i was incapable of fitting this
ghastly description. right?! they knew it, right? he
knew that, right?

if he did, he pretended to have forgotten on that day.

i sat there unable to think of anything other than
the fact that my 'good intentions' had been totally
disregarded. i mean, not one mention was made
of how i was actually a good person. no one made
mention of my heart. i was screaming on the inside,
and i wanted to yell out, "but what about my heart?!"
apparently, only god knew about that.

that was the first time i consciously understood that
my intentions really didn't matter. it did not matter
that i hadn't intended to hurt anyone. all that mattered

was that i had hurt someone.

so began yet another journey for me: finding contentment in the fact that only god would ever really know my heart, and getting over the fact that people were so easy to forget. that was a tough one.

i mean, i cried about it. i cried because i couldn't accept someone believing something about me that was so far from the truth. especially someone who knew me better than that!! ugh! (it makes me shudder even still) yes, i made a detrimental mistake and broke someone's heart. that being said, i would have handled the situation completely different if the shoe was on the other foot. i say that with the most solid confidence. i'm different. yes, i'm different.

i don't think it's okay to pretend to forget about someone's heart. when people hurt others, there is a secreted reason underneath it all. compassionate, forgiving people seek the cause. they don't become victims, and feel like "how dare you do this to me?" as if they are exempt from the pitfalls of life. and they surely don't spitefully slander a person's name or lie about them seeking some sort of futile vengeance. i would never do that. i wouldn't.

that, too, is why i cried.

i handle people's hearts with tender love and care. i'm a non-judgmental person when it comes to matters of the heart. i'm an understanding and forgiving person, because i know that there is no such thing as a perfect human. including myself.

truths. and freedom

but that is only who i intend to be.

and i understand now, that good intentions are not always enough. not for most people. maybe not for anyone, i don't know.

for the most part, i have gotten over being misunderstood in the situation. a lot of the problem was that i just needed to totally forgive myself.

an even bigger feat was accepting that god had totally forgiven me. ah...

that was my biggest hurdle. even though i knew that he forgives. i still just held on to so much guilt. i couldn't get over letting him down, and that made me feel unworthy; unlovable. i think i was concerning myself with others' opinions of me in an effort to hold off dealing with what god's opinion of me was.

it was in those quiet moments that i was able to deal with the real issues. once everyone was gone and the voices stopped. i had to face him.

he was all that mattered. and once i faced him, i found so much peace.

i was facing something so ugly, so complicated, so not reflective of my intentions or character. there were three simple things that kept me through it all:
he loves me. he likes me. i'm his.

moments.

that moment when you're drowning and reaching out for the very person you'd give your life for. they're standing there. you're crying out. they hear you. they see you. but won't save your life.

i've lived that moment.

i hate to think back on it, because the pain resurfaces. i'll never forget.

i swear i could feel my heart breaking into a million pieces.

he refused to come to my rescue. he chose not to defend me, but rather to assault my character. it broke me. i've never felt so rejected. he was not the only one against me, but he was the only one that mattered.
i still think about it. still have images of him walking away as i drowned in turmoil.
ever been abandoned?

i finally want to talk about it. i don't care to conceal that truth anymore.

let me explain:
my sweet daughter is no surprise to her biological father or me. we had relations on and off for nearly a decade. we shared an equally strong desire for one another. it was very sexual, yes, but there was also this conversation piece. we made love with words. we were both lovers of the pictures we could paint with them. the colors were extremely enticing.

truths. and freedom

i loved him, and he knew it. i loved him more than anyone. he knew it. i loved him more than my ex-husband. they both knew it. yes, my ex as well. i risked so much, because i loved him.
the heart can be deceiving.

when i exposed the truth about my daughter belonging to him, i became his nemesis over night. i don't know what i thought would happen, but i know i didn't think that being left to fend for myself was on the list of options.

i didn't get it. let me tell you something. that hurt. badly.

i had him on one end painting me out to be some sort of gold digging groupie.

on the other end, there was my soon to be ex-husband playing the woeful victim as if this was all so surprising to him. as if we hadn't been seeing a therapist since within the first year of our marriage.

as if i hadn't told him that i was not in love with him during that time. as if he didn't know that i'd only stayed in the marriage because i couldn't stand to break his heart.

i mean. that was a lot. i had fingers pointing from all directions.

everything was my fault. everything. no one else accepted any blame. it all felt unfair, but i mainly couldn't get past the fact that the person who had actively participated in the act, the other half of the matter, had turned against me.

fast forward.

we're all three in the courtroom together: two angry men and a crying woman. wow. i was the murderer. they were the casualties.

they both presented the same argument: she acted alone.

i remember taking the stand. their eyes glared through me, reflecting the pieces of my shattered heart.

i broke down. i couldn't take being there like that. where does love go? how does it so quickly disappear?

i don't operate that way. if i've ever loved you, i'll always love you. i don't turn off just because things didn't turn out the way i'd hoped. i don't stop caring about someone just because they don't turn out to be who i thought they were.

we're only human. none of us perfect. none of us deserving to be left out in the cold. all of us needing acceptance. forgiveness. all of us needing unconditional love.

these men completely left me out to dry. it needs to be said that they were both cowards. they didn't stand up as men and admit their role in any of it. i stood there, shameful, though i was, and admitted to my wrong doings. i put it all on the table, because i was brave

truths. and freedom

enough to do so. i didn't allow people's perception of me to deter me from finding out if the truth could in fact set me free. and i refused to allow my frustration with them to destroy my integrity; i would not diminish them as human beings just for the sake of preserving my own good image.

i took it all. i never once said a negative thing about either of them. i could have, but that's not a part of my make up. i wanted to at times, but i could never justify it. there was no gain for me. the most i'll say is that they behaved as only a coward would. when you allow someone else to take the fall for you, that's what you're reduced to in my book.

and well, this is my book.

ruin as a gift.

i marvel at things that have survived ruin. what i wouldn't give to stand inside the once unstoppable ancient roman empire, or gaze upon the beauty that is classical greece. i'd love to inquire about the minds of the people with tour guides at the astonishing mayan ruins.

i'd like to see the pyramids in giza for myself. i'm mind blown by their structure alone, but then i consider the people who built them, the strength it required, the tools they invented, the time and effort put into creating something lasting.

i could go on about the ruins in turkey, italy, jordan, china, israel, and zimbabwe, or i could simply speak on new york. it's nowhere near as old as the places mentioned above, however, its old, ruined, yet breathtaking splendor inspires millions daily. visitors come and gawk at tarnished walls and decaying buildings. there is character and history at every corner. it's hauntingly beautiful and stirring.

we are indeed fascinated by ruin. maybe it's the mere fact that these structures still exist, and that something that could have been reduced to nothing is still here. we see the lasting effect. we see that glory can be found in just standing.

there is brilliance and beauty in just standing.
we marvel at things that stand.
the test of time.
time itself is a test.

truths. and freedom

we pass the test by standing.
facing ruin, yes, at times.
but still standing.
and knowing.
that when it's all over, everything will be beautiful.
beautiful.
stand and be beautiful.
it's beautiful to still be standing when it's all said and done.

and beyond all that, you know what can be taken from the beauty of ruin? the fact that the ruin itself shows. it is revealed; not hidden.

what if the columns at the parthenon in ancient greece were not stained with the remnants of literally being burned by the persians? would the draw be the same if we could not see the decomposition, the battle wounds, the evidence of survival?

i'd argue that we would pay it little mind. we'd admire it for a short time, but we would soon forget. we marvel at those things that have a story and depth to them, because they make us feel something. they remind us that we're not alone in the complexities and layers of our lives.

so from ruined things we learn that we need not hide our imperfections, our stains, our marks. if we do, we forfeit some of our beauty.

listen, here's the thing. here's what i'm getting at: whatever it is. whatever has felt like ruin in your life can be beautiful if you let it. given time (and yes, that's

the hard part), but also strength and lasting power
everything you've been through will be beautiful. i
know it can feel awful when your life is in ruin, but
really it's just going through a transformation, you
know? it's changing into something that will be so
glorious, have so much character, offer a story, inspire
someone, be lasting, and offer an example of how
beautiful it is to stand.
to survive.

when it's all said and done, i just want to be standing.
yes, i will have endured a lot. i will have bent and
swayed through the storms i've faced. i will have scars
and bruises from hits that really took something out
of me. i will have felt like the end must be near several
times over. i will have almost given in, i will have
almost crumbled…

but.
i will have decided in the midst of my darkest nights,
bowed over in the middle of those hurtful places that
no matter what i might endure, i will survive.

i will not die, or cease to exist because of ruin. and i
will not stop standing in what will surely become all
of my glory. i will forfeit zero layers of my beauty. i will
not lay down.

i will stand here and last through the test of time.
author's note:

ruin is a gift, because it allows god to be glorified
through us. it is his strength that gives us resilience.

truths. and freedom

we need him to survive. please… don't give in. stand tall in the face of ruin. it is the road to transformation.

what you are becoming is so much better than what you are right now! embrace the journey of transformation. it's going to be beautiful!

i was walking through my house yesterday, and i thought to myself: "i am literally walking in my story right now. even the parts that don't feel so good are making for a great piece of work. so, i think i'll just keep going and see how it turns out… i have a feeling it'll be something to marvel at."

i felt my shoulders go back after that thought. the corners of my mouth even turned upwards. a breath escaped me. it was one that needed to be released.

forgiving me.

forgiveness is a journey.

i have been on the journey for quite some time now.

when i was a young girl, i had to forgive my daddy. he didn't always know exactly how to nurture me emotionally. over and over i had to forgive him. i used to hate that i understood the significance of forgiveness, because truthfully there were times i didn't want to forgive. but i knew i had to. i've been forgiving people for a long time with no problem: church folk, friends, foes, outsiders, insiders, family members, etc. for me, forgiveness was relatively easy. i guess i was kind of good at it.

until i had to forgive myself.

forgiving me was an especially long journey. i was so lost inside of self-sorrow and regret. i could not see the good within myself anymore. i became numb to life, feelings, and emotions. it was the only way i could live with myself. i was on serious auto-pilot. serious pretend mode.

i knew that god was capable of forgiving me, but i think... i felt too bad to even ask him to. i didn't want to have to ask god to forgive me for something that i should have never let happen. i was too ashamed of myself to face him. i now know why. so, i'd gotten myself into this whole ordeal because i hadn't taken the time to seek him in the first place. i was only consulting with myself when it came to making

truths. and freedom

decisions. i hadn't asked for his help then, so what gave me the right to call on him now. he shouldn't have to save me from myself when my self should have allowed him to protect me from the very beginning.

time.

it seems bigger when you're in it. more impossible. longer. harder. while you're going through. our troubles are magnified and seemingly endless as we endeavor to find our way out of them. they are always bigger from the inside looking out.

i'm beginning to understand the rhythm of life. the ebb and flow of it all. the high and low tides that come and then go. come and then go. i recognize that there is a sure pattern even within the seasons of our lives. there is a rhythm, and i am slowly beginning to feel its pulse.

know its cadence.

one thing that is certain about time: it goes on.

looking back on some of the things i've faced, i recall how big they seemed while i was on the inside looking out. i nearly drowned myself in worry, because i just couldn't visualize how everything was going to work out for me. in my heart, i believed it would, but it felt like it might take forever... i worried that forever was too long.

i think i've often viewed time as my enemy. it can be so deceptive. it moves fast and also slow. and always opposite of what you wish. when you're at a low point in life, it seems time stands still. and at the high points, you wish it would slow down.

all the time, the cadence is unchanging. the pulse remains the same. it keeps going. on and on.

truths. and freedom

my concern was always time. being stuck in a situation will allow you to hear it passing all around you. i was enveloped in its echoes–tick tock...tick tock.

freedom from within.

no one can give freedom to you. it comes from within.
and for the same reason, no one can take it away.

freedom begins with truth, continues in righteousness,
and in the end leaves you feeling
unbound.

i often ask myself what it is about me that makes
people believe i'm so free. i mean, clearly i talk about
the topic a lot in my writing, but other than that i'm
just out here living a pretty normal life. i'm not going
or doing any and everything i please. i have a job,
a child, and responsibilities like anybody else. my
calendar is full and i get overwhelmed just like the
next person, so what is it? what do people see?

it's really so simple when i stop and consider it, and i
get it. it's easy.
they see me, transparently.
i walk in truth.

people appreciate and gravitate towards transparency
and rawness. while it is one's prerogative to be an
open book, we know that those are the people we
are most compelled to. i love a person that can sit
down and make no qualms about the fact that she's
gone through, and 'been there'. you know? like, i
immediately love her. she's raw and rare. she's genuine
and beautiful. her head is high in confidence and
wisdom, not hung in shame or guilt.

it may be hard to believe, but i love being transparent

truths. and freedom

for several reasons:
for one, it's a release. i don't want to keep things balled up inside. i'd much rather let them escape me. i literally want to get it out, so that it's no longer in me. do you understand? like, i want it out of me. i don't want to carry it around. writing is the best way i know to do that.

secondly, i like being the one to tell my story. there are lots of layers to my life, and i'm sure people get a lot wrong when they're relaying it (for whatever reason) to others. i like to think i take matters into my own hands by speaking on my own experiences. i'll be the first to admit, they're pretty interesting. it's a pretty 'colorful' story to say the least.

but here's the big thing for me. what i love most about being an open book is: my truth encourages people who may be struggling with their own truth. being transparent allows people around me to feel comfortable being and doing the same. i can't tell you how many exchanges i've had with people where we've discussed their skeletons openly. sometimes i've barely (if ever) even met them. folk open right up, (i believe) because they feel safe and don't fear judgment. it's a wonderful thing! what if none of us feared judgment from others? can you imagine being that free?

what a relief to be unreserved even for a minute!

i am relieved to be unreserved and honest about who i really am and what i've been through. daily, my life is lighter because i'm not carrying around anything heavy that stresses me. i'm not concerned about people knowing my imperfections. like, it actually makes me feel better to know that people know i'm not perfect.

some would say i share too much, yet they gravitate towards the stories i tell. they don't agree with me putting out so much of my personal life, yet they want to know more.

there is something that we are all drawn to, and it's called the truth. consider the ease you have when you know you're being told the truth. it allows you to drop your guard and exist at ease.
i don't want to be perceived as perfect, or a person who has it all together, because i'm not and i don't. and that is a lot of pressure that i don't need. you know? plus, i know it's needed.

we are all fed perfection on a regular basis. it's a disease in our society. people go and alter their whole bodies because they see imperfection in their reflection. similarly, people hide their internal flaws by pretending to be someone they're not.

in our world everything is supposed to be flawless from image to home to work and beyond. people like to walk around as if there's nothing wrong. what?! everything is wrong it seems! so, we need more raw people who make it okay to not be perfect all the time. we never will be! and that's okay. '

planted.

eventually, the desire to understand our own layers deepens. some dig in and do the dirty work, getting down to the root of who they really are.

some prefer not to bother what's below for fear of altering what appears to be thriving above the surface.

what i have found is this: in getting down to the roots, we're able to better understand what may be necessary for a thing to grow.

it's simple. if i don't know the names and origins of the seeds that were planted, i am unable to properly nurture them. i'm unaware of the type of soil they thrive in. how much sunlight is enough or too much? water daily, or weekly?

you see, there are things that, if understood, will allow a thing to live and thrive as it is meant to. and there are things that, if never understood, can prevent the thing from ever blooming as beautifully as it should.

it's hard for me to accept that proper growth can happen without first understanding the characteristics of the seed that was planted, the things that took root, and the growth that happened or didn't happen as a result of its environment.

what if the person we see in the mirror is only an under nurtured version of who we're really supposed to be?

what if we haven't been tended to properly, simply because no one (including ourselves) ever took the time to dig deeply and understand what we have the potential of becoming.

why doesn't anyone wanna dig? seems most folk would rather just pour on more dirt and bury, bury, bury.

i'm speaking metaphorically here, but we know that is never the answer. don't we?

no amount of covering is going to fix what's going on underneath it all. and, you know? it could be that there's absolutely nothing wrong underneath the surface. but i still believe it's better to know. to be aware. to recognize what is in us.

what if there are things you haven't tapped into yet, because you didn't know you could?

my point is this: get to know your kind. know thyself. come up from the dirt if you have to, and get grounded in fresh soil. the kind of soil that's just right for you.

the kind of soil that will allow you to take root and grow tall and strong. take the time to figure out how much sunlight you require. how often you should be watered. pay attention to the environments you thrive best in. identify your good seeds, and nurture them, and dig up the bad ones before they take root. if they already have, pull them up. tug, chop, cut, break, and work unremittingly to rid yourself of their blight.

truths. and freedom

do whatever you must to become the best version of yourself. the complete you. the full you. the you that reveals the brilliant spectrum of your true colors.

this has been my pursuit for well for a while now, and my only regret is that i didn't really know to do it sooner. i'm nothing like the person i thought i was.

actually, i'm much more like the person i thought i wasn't.

has it been dirty getting down to my truths, my seeds, my purpose? yeah, it has at times. but the growth that's happened since is so worth it. now that i know who i am underneath it all, i've began to truly thrive.

i mean, like thrive in a new way. this way feels real. it feels fresh. healthy. right.

ebb and flow.

there is an ebb and flow. it is uninterrupted. the rhythm sometimes varies, but it is continuous.

there are highs. highs like love, happiness (based on circumstance), good finances, great relationships with family and people in general, career goals being met, feeling organized, newness, fresh starts, travel, valuable learning, enriching experiences, feeling important, order.

and there are lows. lows like rejection, abandonment, confusion, indecisiveness, loneliness, doubt, break-ups, deaths, unexpected change, financial trouble, debt, sickness, the loss of loved ones, being unsure, fear of the unknown, issues at work, bad relationships, desperation.

these highs and lows will come and go just as sure as there is night, and there is day.

with this most valuable understanding i do two things:

stay humble when things are amazing. and remain hopeful when things seem hopeless.

the process is not easy initially, but with time, lessons, and practice it becomes possible. for me, it's not only possible, but necessary. necessary because i refuse to go through life feeling like i deserve to be happy all the time when i do so many things that make me unworthy of that. on the other hand, i refuse to go through life beat down when i have a merciful god who orders my steps and in whom i place my trust.

so.
i stay humble when things are amazing, because i have knowledge of life's ebb and flow. i get that things could take a turn for the worse at any moment. but. when they do i don't stay down for long. ever. whatever it is, i let it hurt. i feel and release the emotions that i need to, and then i wait with great hope for that ebb and flow to raise me up again. in the meantime i reflect on the blessing of lessons, and how they grow me up. i take the time to appreciate the wisdom, and then... well, and then i write them all down.

the thing about being who we are.

"i was once afraid of people saying, 'who does she think she is?' now i stand and say, 'this is who i am.'" –oprah

i absolutely love this! it is the story of my life in a basic little line. simply put, it is the evolution from girl to woman. it is a truism for any evolving woman. it is the #struggle. it is the triumph!

standing and saying those words to the world is the most freeing and liberating feeling i've ever experienced. "this is who i am."

owning and loving myself for everything that i am and am not, oh my god... it's why i write. it's why i share.

it's what i hope to inspire women to do for themselves: to discover how beautiful they are, and how much more beautiful they are because of their victories in life. to know that there is no victory without #struggle.

and to understand that the #struggle makes us smarter, sharper, more capable, wiser, and better.

and most importantly, that we are all so connected, so similar, so linked in our journeys.

we have more in common than we dare to consider, but we're too busy focusing on the things that separate us. if we would only open our eyes, our mind, and hearts. we are surrounded by beauty. power.

truths. and freedom

intelligence. strength. experience. wisdom. knowledge. truth. compassion. and most of all, love.

regardless of where we've individually come from, we are all built the same. we are cut from the same cloth and carry a common thread that fuses us all together.

and if the truth be told, we are similar not in spite of our differences, but because of them.

"this is who i am," when said with conviction, can be the most powerful statement of one's life.

once, a girlfriend of mine enlightened me:
i was speaking of my past indiscretions and how they truly could have ruined my name. i also shared how perfectly aware i am of how awful the scenario must have looked to outsiders. her response was so matter of fact. she said, "yeah, but you don't leave any room for judgment, brandie. you carry no lingering shame, and so it doesn't allow people to dwell on it either. you're like, yeah that happened... this is what i learned... let's move on, shall we?."

i'd never thought of it like that. i'd never considered where i might be had i never owned up to, confessed, and released the guilt of my poor decisions. i might still be living in the aftermath of something that happened years ago.

i imagine there are people that way. stuck in the same guilt. the same blame. the same shame of years passed. they've never broken free of that. they don't know how.

here's the secret:
forgive yourself.
forgive yourself.
no, really, forgive yourself for not being perfect.

i could stop right here and have a good cry, because from the moment my mistake happened i carried a burden so heavy. and i carried it all alone. it weighed and weighed on me until i had to release it, or be consumed by it. it. was. hard. to forgive myself.

honestly, one of the hardest things i've ever had to do. to make my mind stop reminding me of what a horrible thing i'd done.

even worse? i couldn't accept god's forgiveness, either.

i knew that he would forgive me, but it's like i just couldn't accept his offer. i'd think, "no, god, you're too generous. i know you're saying i can have it, but i just can't. i can't accept this from you. thanks, but i... i just don't deserve it."

pause. feeling the tears burn now.

that's a hard place to be. i get it. i get how you get stuck there. but you have to decide that you're not going to allow your imperfections, your mistakes, your past... to define who you are ultimately going to be. you're going to be incredible. you're going to be extraordinary. you're going to be someone's amazing wife, mother, friend, nurturer, teacher, or whatever it is you're going to be...
i had to start believing that more than i believed i was

truths. and freedom

unforgivable.

once i forgave myself, and accepted god's forgiveness
things really began to makes sense to me.
the acceptance piece was huge. huge!
i not only accepted my imperfections, but also
acknowledged them as the most ordinary part
of me. that acknowledgment freed my mind of
unwanted thoughts of people's criticisms towards
me. i once again understood my worth. i thought to
myself, "i mean, if god still loves me, clearly, i am of
distinguished value."

my confidence increased. my compassion grew more
christ-like. my self-awareness matured.
and then.
i knew and declared,
"this is who i am."
and. no lie…

as opposed to making people turn away…
those words drew more people to me than i ever
imagined. i was suddenly made acutely aware of how
akin we all are. my openness allowed others to feel
safe enough to do the same. i realized just how much
we need each other.

i am amazed daily at how all things work together for
our good. completely amazed.
if only we could all begin to accept it all: the good, the
bad, the ugly, and the in-between.
if we could stop worrying about people saying, "who
does she think she is…"

we would all be living, freely, as exactly who we are!

the bottom line is this: look in the mirror first. and don't look with a biased lens simply because it's you. be real with yourself about who you really are. how do you treat people? how do you handle your relationships? when you are not your best self, do you admit that? how do you treat yourself, and in what ways are you growing? are you making an effort to grow, or are you satisfied with yourself so much so that you are content?

the few of us, though, who have stopped placing blame and started to look inward… oh, we're the wise ones. we're the ones who have the rare gift to see beauty in everything. yes, even the ugly stuff. and we don't miss a lesson. we make it a point to find it in every situation. we have come to the understanding that god doesn't waste a hurt.

i thank god for the gift.

let it hurt.

confusion (noun):

1. lack of understanding; uncertainty.
2. a situation of panic; a breakdown of order.

being lost within a maze of confusion can be the most fear-provoking experience of one's existence.

being fearful prevents forward movement. steps are extremely hesitant. guards go up in preparation for cover. hearts pound with a burdensome heaviness.

confusion casts an ominous darkness. depression lurks nearby. silence goes off like a siren.

this is why i'd rather not think things through. i don't want to get to that place of confusion that happens when i think too much. being over-analytical is not often a characteristic that i enjoy owning. rather, it is a trait that sends me into endless spirals of thought and indecisiveness.

it's easiest to hold on to what i already have a grasp of (because it's familiar), as opposed to letting go.
letting go...

what do i do when it hurts?

let it hurt. just let it.

just because it hurts doesn't mean i'm going to die. sometimes the only way to overcome something is to let life take its course and do its work. it might break me. it might take me down to my knees... interestingly enough, it's in those moments when i'm broken and on my knees that i seek truth desperately. on my knees in surrender, my guards are down. i am no longer afraid. my heart is calm and order is restored.

honestly, i want to stay there in submission to his will for my life. comfort engulfs me. tears flow freely, and somehow i am able to see so clearly through them. out flows my cares, concerns, and uncertainties. i am safe.

i remain on my knees as long as possible. once i stand, it'll be up to me to take the first step to get out of the maze.

we don't want to hurt, but it's a part of life. there's really no getting around it. we bypass the hardest routes in life because we anticipate all the bumps and potholes. we instead take an alternative road, which will ultimately lead us to the same place; it'll just take longer. i'm even convinced that the alternative road is one huge circle that leads right back to the hard route that we were trying to avoid.

all because we're too afraid to make a decision.

in other words: there are things in life we just have to face. some of those things will just be flat out hard. it's going to hurt. why put if off? when we know what we have to do, we have got to learn to forget about our fears and just do it.

i can recall being so lost and just having no

truths. and freedom

understanding whatsoever. i didn't understand how one decision could just completely turn my life upside-down.

i learned to just let it hurt.

i would go home and i'd cry it out. i'd punch the pillow and then scream into it. i'd fall out on the floor and roll around like a person who'd lost all control. finally, i'd end up on my knees in complete surrender. i would just weep and call his name... that's when i'd get that reassurance that i was going to be okay. i took it one day at a time. if i got weak, back down on my knees i'd go. then, here would come that comfort, and i'd get up and try again. one day i emerged from the maze i'd been captive to. i had survived. the pain hadn't killed me.

i have gotten over the fear of making mistakes. i mean, so what if i make them? isn't it one of the most natural things to not always make the right decision? what i figured out is that what matters more is the way i bounce back once i've made the wrong decision. will i linger in the mess of that mistake, or will i pick up the pieces and put myself back together again. i learned to own up to my mistakes as well. they make me more human and more compassionate towards others. they help me to be slow to judge. they make me better. they really do.

getting over the fear of making mistakes or failing in life was huge for me! once i let that fear go, i stopped getting so stuck all the time. i stopped finding myself in the misery that is confusion. accepting my imperfect, mistake prone self was the best thing that i ever did. the way i got to that place was first by owning up to making a huge mess out of my life... and then. making it out alive. more alive than i've ever been.

circles.

i like my life best when i have more answers than questions. uncertainty overwhelms me. it's one of those weaknesses, one of those fears that will quite possibly test me for the rest of my life. i think the issue may be that when i have all the answers i get much too comfortable. i stop seeking and become complacent. i exist safely and contented in my comfort zone... for a while.

but then, inevitably, i look around and begin to loathe the mundane predictability of my life. i begin to search for reasons why and question everything. and everyone. and i drive myself near insanity trying to find answers. during that time, i live on edge in a state of rebellion. until, somehow, just before i completely lose it, i come to myself and return to my safe place.

the place that sometimes offers answers, but all the time offers peace. the place where i find certainty that i will be okay.

the place where i can surrender.
the place where i fall to my knees.

pressing forward.

it continues.

the expedition. the journey. the discovery. the mission. the quest.

i don't have it all figured out. i'm not all put together yet. i'm still searching, learning, and thirsting for more.

i have good days that feel much like all the pieces have come together, and i have not so good days that feel much like the opposite. i've learned how to cope with both: on good days i consciously thank god and deeply consider how good he really is. on not so good days i allow myself to be in that moment also. if i feel the need to cry, then i do. i've come to realize that i need a good cry on average every four to six weeks. seriously.

or i write. like tonight.

i'm currently feeling some kind of way about things. i can't pen-point exactly what it is. it could be one thing or several little things that i've bottled up inside.

i've checked my calendar; it's not pms. by the time i complete this entry, i will feel lighter. i will have figured it out. the tightness in my chest will have subsided. my breathing will have returned to normal.

actually, i can feel the tension already beginning to loosen. writing is a release for me. like crying, it helps me feel better once i get it all out.

truths. and freedom

since my divorce i've suffered from anxiety. it comes in the form of hypertension, migraines, and dizziness.

my body no longer responds to stress well. what i used to consider little issues have become major things for me. i mean, i have found myself sick at times worrying about things that i have zero control over. like, really sick. passed out on the floor -sick.

my divorce was ugly. like, sitting in a court room defending myself against not one, but two men. both present in the hearing. the whole thing lasted nearly a year. i learned more than i ever cared to know about the court system and family law. i handled it mostly on my own and coped mostly by crying. only a little writing occurred during that period. the emotional effects still linger in every migraine. i'm still not completely over how i felt sitting alone in that chair facing what i was facing. i think i have resentment left over from feeling forsaken by both individuals.

but tonight.
it's more about thirst, i think.

i want more out of life and my mouth is watering, because i can taste it. i feel like i'm at a critical point in my life, maybe even on the brink of something big.

i can sense that things are shifting in my favor, so i'm bracing myself for the road blocks that are sure to appear.

i still seek wisdom. more and more of it. i want to become more committed. committed to god, his word, and will for me. committed to myself and my health.

committed to my dreams. committed to people and god's work for me.

maybe that's what tonight is about. i don't feel like i'm succeeding at all the things i want to do and be. yes.

that's it. i am being overcritical of myself. i feel like i'm failing. i'm in my feelings. historically, when i get like this it causes me to give up, because fear sets in. the last thing i want to be in life is a failure, so the safest thing has always been to just quit before i become that.

crazy thing is, if it were anyone else i would advise them to keep pressing.

well tonight, i will remind myself to press towards the mark for the prize of the high calling in jesus christ.

i will encourage myself that it will all be worth it.

everything i've been through, everything i'm learning about myself, every night that i've sat wanting and thirsting for more. it will be made manifest when i reach my destination.

and just like that. i feel better...

i'm actually sitting here smiling (and here come the tears—of joy now), because...
i'm getting there.

slowly, yes, but surely. and at the end of the day,

truths. and freedom

whether it was a good one or not, i have only two options: keep moving or don't.

at the end of today, i choose to keep moving.

a brand new kind of free.

i talk a lot about being free. the word encompasses so much for me; i don't know if i could ever give it a complete explanation. i can only share partial illustrations and experiences that have lead me to the feeling.
lately though,

as i grow older there's this sense of urgency/fear looming over me. all of a sudden i feel as if i'm running out of time to live the life i always dreamed of. in addition, watching the news causes me to believe the world is nearing its end. seriously. i am all too aware of time. i am anxious. anxious is never good.

recently, i've had the time to just be still. my thoughts have been all over the place where my future is concerned. i have been caught up on my career, finances, gifts/talents and what to do with them, etc. i've been beating myself up a bit about opportunities i feel i've missed out on. i almost discouraged myself from continuing my aspirations in music. i was beginning to feel like i don't really have a voice (both literally and figuratively) that will pierce the soul. i want to make people feel something. i want to inspire good in people. i want to spread love.

i was feeling down about fulfilling a purpose on this earth. i was praying and asking god to give me clarity concerning his plan for me. i needed a clear direction.

and i needed peace and faith about it. and i needed drive and motivation. i was asking for a lot, i felt. and

i was asking for things i felt i should already have and know. so, in other words, i almost felt guilty for even having to ask.
and then.

i heard something that changed my viewpoint.
it caused me to ask myself a simple question:
how have i been measuring my success?

what has been my aim on a daily basis? when i wake up in the morning i immediately begin checking things off my never ending list. the first way to quantify my success for the day is whether or not i do all the things that are part of my morning routine and make it out of the house on time.

anxiety starts before the sun even comes up.
it doesn't end until i've "successfully" fed, bathed, and put my child to bed at a decent time. only then can i begin to determine whether my day was successful.

did i do this? did i remember that? all these questions and lists flood my brain and are used to determine whether i was successful that day.
and that's just the surface!

if i get an opportunity to stop and think about the grand scheme of my success, the questions are even more abundant: am i where i'm supposed to be? am i doing what i'm supposed to be doing? should i be making more money? how does my success compare to that of my peers? when will i ever truly feel successful?

this question caused me to want to change my perspective. big time. it challenged me to throw my old idea of success out the door.

i no longer want success.

i want to marvel at something. at life. i want to measure my life in wonder.

i want to wake up in wonder. i want to be excited about what the day might bring. i want to live in anticipation; not anxiety. i want to look forward to what my life will bring about; not worry about what it won't deliver.

i realized that i had to change my way of thinking so that i could become even freer than before. i desire a life that is free of urgency, anxiety, and the fear of time and failure. caring about success brings about all of that.

so i am setting out on a new journey. more self-discovery. i'm excited!

i've decided that there are different stages of freedom. my twenties offered countless lessons that gave me the courage to be brandie, freely, and reveal my truest self. i learned how the truth sets you free.

in that level i broke free. in this next level of freedom i wanna discover how to fly. i wanna truly learn to spread my wings and allow them to be beautiful. the way god created them. if i have to fall a couple of times, i'm willing to. it'll only make me better. i'm gonna push myself to the limit and run full speed ahead until i lift

truths. and freedom

off. i'll take the risk and jump. i've got to. if i plan to fly. and i do plan to fly. it's one step closer to being able to soar. oh, to be up there marveling at the new heights god will allow me to see. i wanna live in awe of his glory. let it be revealed in me.

no more success. just wonder. i wanna wake up in it.

instead of being concerned about how many my voice might reach, i'm just going to use it. because i would be living beneath my privilege to not use a gift that the creator freely gave to me. instead of worrying about having a best seller, i'm just going to write. because i love it. it helps me if no one else.

no more measuring success, because the weight of failure prevents me from flying.
and i want to fly.

i want to reach new heights.

wonder > success

brandie freely

freedoms.

words and thoughts i live by.

the significance of your
arrival will be short lived
but what learnings you collect
on the journey
will maintain value
long after.

truths. and freedom

the truth.
can still penetrate.
can still pierce the surface.
without being catapulted
from your tongue
like a furious blade.

forgiveness is a gift to the forgiver.

truths. and freedom

there are two types:
those who settle
and those who don't.
and that's only an observation.
everyone has their reasons.
neither is wrong. or right. perhaps.
just very different existences.

brandie freely

there are some things you can't feel
until you're numb.

truths. and freedom

for we know that
the seed of every ending
sprouts a new
beginning.

don't let gravity keep you down.

truths. and freedom

not all good things are meant to last forever
just because they're good.

it's okay to let go of something good sometimes.
and it's okay to believe for and await
something better.

everything was different.
she could feel the shift in the core of her being.
it was time.
so, a lantern she lit.
and into the unknown she stepped
praying
father, keep me.

know that letting go is never the end.

pack light.
and
pack light.

truths. and freedom

do the best you can. continue to learn yourself. love yourself. forgive yourself and others. know that letting go isn't the end. accept the past as it is. move on. find reasons to be grateful. don't carry too much. have hope. keep going. be light. pack light. be free. go higher.

no one. nothing. ever leaves you.
we're made up of our experiences, each one.
so, embrace them all.

truths. and freedom

time is a healer.

be clean in the way you do things.
you will have to deal with the mess you create.
usually on your own.

stillness can take you far.

and even if i could've chosen the woman i wanted to be.
i would've chosen the woman
i see
right now
 in this mirror.

truths. and freedom

truth is:
i need to be the woman that
you and i
both want.

i want to fall in love so organically,
so sincerely,
so authentically
that i'm surprised
the day the words fall from lips.
like, wow,
it's been you all the time.

truths. and freedom

feel it all.
feel it all. let it hurt. let it make you happy all over.
let it fill you. let it deplete you.
whatever it is,
feel it
so you can forever remember what it taught you.
the lesson is so important.

brandie freely

what if
the times we stumble and fall
are what allow
us to duck
and dodge
the bullets flying over
our
heads?

truths. and freedom

so he goes from place to place
collecting pieces
he thinks
will put him back
together again.
and it
never works,
because he must first
find his own peace.

brandie freely

...and i knew that i was not the cause of that light, that i wasn't the only person that has seen that in her, that there was nothing special about me and that it was all about her. and for the first time ever i felt a very unselfish appreciation for it. like watching an orange and blue sun set knowing that sun will still set and be orange and blue whether i am there to see it or not

-from a love letter addressed to me

truths. and freedom

if when you open your hand
it blows away,
let it.
allow the thing the choice to stay
or go.

forget the american dream
remember your own.

truths. and freedom

don't allow the way the experience ended
to be the thing the experience is
defined by.
much more is lost that way.
much less is gained.

brandie freely

keep all the good stuff.
hide it like treasure
within you.

truths. and freedom

"this is who i am"
when said with conviction can be the most powerful proclamation of your life.

the only way to see things clearly is by keeping your lenses clean.

you can't focus on the future when finger prints from days passed are clouding your view.

truths. and freedom

stop shaping your future
using a man
as the mold.

i'm a glass vase. someone dropped me once.
i broke apart,
but all my pieces were still there.

i found some extra strength glue and put myself back together.

same vase, but with an interesting story.

it's not that i'm afraid of someone picking me up again, i just need to be sure the hands are strong and steady enough, and that they'll carry me to a home that will treasure me forever.

but even before then, i need to take care of my breaks. i'm fragile now, but i won't be forever. maybe a passerby will notice me in the window and keep coming back until i'm ready
to come home.

-in repair

truths. and freedom

greatness was within her. buried. hidden. but alive.
and she couldn't have known
had she not kept going down
a path
of uncertainties
and disappointments.
had she stopped. ever. her
greatness would have gone
unrealized. had she not continued
moving.
it might have died.

truth is:
i feel more beautiful as
a survivor.
staring at my reflection in the complete nude.
battle wounds exposed.
i am deeply pleased
by what i still look like.

truths. and freedom

honestly, i'm grateful to have lived the
american dream.
because now i know
i ain't missin much.

currently you're
in my rear view.
eventually
even that will fade.

truths. and freedom

the most rare
and sought after flowers are
planted in particularly rich soil.
understand.
dirt can cause
you
to bloom more beautifully.

brandie freely

sometimes i'm in a mood for vibrant colors and
interesting unbalance.

and other times i need muted or even dark colors and
simple, clean lines.

you know? sometimes i don't mind being melancholy.
and other times i need good vibes only.

i'm thankful for it all. all my feelings. all my
experiences. my whole life.
the dull and the colorful.
i'm thankful that i have learned to appreciate it all.

truths. and freedom

i want to make more memories than plans.

maybe her love was too much for him to hold.
maybe his heart wasn't wide enough
maybe her love was meant for more than one heart.
maybe it was meant for the world.
maybe she was wider than her own imagination.
maybe she was much more than she knew, he knew, they knew.
maybe her love was meant for the world. maybe her love.
maybe her.
she.
was much, much
more.

truths. and freedom

what drives me
is the fear of being on my death bed with a long list of regrets.
i don't care what it is, how big or small.
the fear can no longer be failure.
the fear must be having never tried at all.

there are some things you just have to leave behind.
even if it's the very thing
you don't want to do.

truths. and freedom

may you sleep in peace.
may regret never consume you.
for we're all on a journey to find out who we really are.
may you reach home safely.
may your own light guide you.

-to anyone i've ever loved

if you only knew how my
heart has been broken to pieces,
then you'd understand
how extremely
amazing it is that
i'm stil here,
going on and living and such.

truths. and freedom

i am ever amazed at how time,
when allowed,
can do so much.
it is truly of the essence.
if only i could master seeing life as the whole clock,
instead
of getting stuck in
the many little
seconds in time.

all the while,
the things she truly desired and always loved
never changed.
never left her heart.
they just grew stronger,
silently within,
waiting until she stopped worrying about
whether or not they made any sense.
waiting until she fully released her every inhibition
and became everything
she was ever meant to be.

truths. and freedom

it is necessary to do what's right no matter what.
and that is not always easy.
but do it.
not for praise or admiration,
but simply because right is right.

you will never have control over
the unknown.

truths. and freedom

it's not usually a matter of knowing what to do;
it's doing what you know.

i'm good at accepting what is,
so moving on is not an issue.
i don't allow good memories to bring on sorrow,
and i don't deny when something was indeed good.
i don't rob myself of the experience nor the lesson.
i understand that for everything there is a season.
so if i've ever loved you, i always will.
if i've ever thought you were good, i won't forget.
if you were ever important to me, you always will be.
i wish you well.
that is the art of freedom.

truths. and freedom

it's a never ending balancing act,
often teetering on the edge of falling all apart.

-life

brandie freely

when soaring above,
a fallen tree does not ruin
the vast beauty of the forest.

truths. and freedom

ruin can bring about beauty.

brandie freely

it was in the moment i revealed my deepest, most
hidden truth
that i found it.
freedom.

truths. and freedom

there is no freedom
without
the absolute
unadulterated
truth.

trusting the process takes practice.

truths. and freedom

january 13, 2014

you were there.
my faith was torn to shreds,
my heart in the balance.
you were there.
always faithful.
always good.

midnight thinking on the mercies of god:

i've lost myself before. more than once. i've felt that god was nowhere near. i've gone far astray. i have.

i've found myself so far gone it felt i'd never get back.

i have done things that i felt were unforgivable. i've struggled with forgiving myself, which made it hard to believe god ever would.

i've struggled in my faith at times. i've wanted answers and have demanded things from god. i've been impatient. i have given up on dreams. misplaced my hope a few times.

i've seen a lot. had my heart broken and broke many hearts. i've been far from perfect. i've let people down.

i've gotten things wrong. i have been dead wrong before.

i've had broken pieces. i've allowed the wrong people to try and put them back together. i've turned to

truths. and freedom

everyone but god before.

i've pretended not to know what's right. i've turned my face. i have.

i've missed opportunities to speak of you. i've been silent when i should have spoken up.

i've spoken in places where i should have been silent. i've ignored your voice. i have not always obeyed.

i thought i had seen the end,
everything broken.
but you were there.
i've wandered at heaven's gates,
and made my bed in hell.
but you were there still...

The lyrics of the song I'm referencing seemed to have come from the very core of my soul.

it's written by michael gungor.

when i reflect on my life, i am so in awe of god's amazing love for me.
always faithful.

always good.
you still have me.
you still have my heart.

that he still loves me.
he still loves me.
loves me.

me.
messed up old me.

his love has changed my life. he has taken it, as dark as it once was, and he is making me into something beautiful. he's changing my life!
he has not given up on me!
he makes all things new.

you know? sometimes we can get so down on ourselves. so low. we can lose sight of the investment we are to god. we are valuable to him. he loves us.

becoming a mother has been the best example of how god can continue to love me. no matter how many times my sweet girl, who's lying right here beside me, may mess up or refuse to follow my voice i would go to the ends of the earth for her.

how much greater is god's love for us?

that's why i'll always find my way back. i will run to his arms, and allow them to be my resting place. my hiding place.

when the world is too cruel. when i can't seem to love myself.

i will think on his everlasting love for me.
and.

i'll love him forever. i make the wrong choices sometimes, but i love him. he loved me first, and i'll love him forever! i am less than perfect, but i love him.

truths. and freedom

his love for me is perfect!
he still has my heart.

now and forever he has my heart.

Xx
b

acknowledgements.

even with a love of words as great as mine, i could never write a sentence beautiful enough to illustrate my deepest gratitude for every person in my life who has led me to this point.

this book is a fifteen year long labor of love and a passion driven work of heart that would have never seen completion were it not for people who believed in me often times more than i believed in myself.

to my daughter, you are the greatest inspiration of my life. i wouldn't be who i am without you. you've made me better in every way. you are the one thing in my whole life that i know, for certain, was meant to be.

i love you, solona elle, and if this is the one and only story i ever tell, i will ever be satisfied knowing that it is the story of you. the story of how you saved my life in perfect time. i love you, my sweet girl.

mama, you're my one thing. my safe place. thank you for teaching me what freedom from within looks like.

you are the most beautiful human i've ever known.

you've loved me enough for two lifetimes. you have kept me alive. i thank god you're mine.

if i attempted to make a list of people to thank, i'd fail.

i'd leave someone really important out, and i'd regret

truths. and freedom

it. and i'd want to reprint the whole book, and it would never be released. ha! just know that from every word, message, email, comment, repost, dm, and all the other advanced ways we have to connect i've received your encouragement, and it has kept me going. to my family and extended family, my mentors, my best friends, my artsy friends, my biggest fans, my students, and fellow educators: thank you for your inspiration and for believing in me.

may you find the courage to dig deep and find your truths and freedom.

Xx
-b

dear reader,

thank you for reading and supporting truths. and freedom.

for an independent author like myself, one of the best ways to gain exposure is through reviews on amazon or audible as well as through sharing information about my work through social media, email, and word of mouth. if you enjoyed and especially gained anything from this book, please write a review on one of the above platforms. there are also ways to share on my website www.brandiefreely.com and/or on social media @ brandiefreely

again, thank you for reading. it means more to me than i could ever express.

                                                          Xx
                                                          -b